# Our Snow Bear Scrapbook

## Memories and Recipes
### from Thalhimers©

Written by
## Elizabeth Thalhimer

Illustrated by
## Sallie Thalhimer

*All proceeds from the sale of Our Snow Bear Scrapbook will go to Theatre IV's arts-in-education programs.*

The Dietz Press
Richmond, Virginia

Library of Congress Card Number: 00-105626

ISBN 0-87517-111-7
Printed in China

Dedicated to

**Barbara and William B. Thalhimer, Jr.**
on the occasion of
his 85th and her 80th birthdays
and their 60th wedding anniversary,
all in 1999

And to

everyone who
worked and shopped at
Thalhimers

On the bookshelf in my room sits my slightly tattered but much-loved Snow Bear who smiles down at me like my oldest friend. My bear and I share fond memories of Thalhimers, the Southern department store chain founded by my great-great-great grandfather in 1842. The story of how Thalhimers began, grew, and evolved into a retail giant is fascinating, but my story is much simpler and spans only sixteen years. All I possess from these years growing up with the store is a series of hazy, delicious memories...and my beloved Snow Bear.

Almost anyone who grew up in Richmond, Virginia remembers the excitement of going downtown to shop during the holidays. It was the time of year when everything seemed to glitter, even the sidewalks down Broad Street. My younger sisters and I always dressed up in matching smocked dresses, black patent leather shoes, and woolen coats with velveteen collars to visit Santa and Snow Bear at the downtown Thalhimers store where Daddy worked. The day was filled with as much giddy anticipation as Christmas morning.

Our day began when Figgus, a jovial valet, parked our car in Dad's spot as we scurried over to the garage corral to pet the majestic police horses. Then Mom gathered us together and, like little ducklings, we paraded towards the store. Holiday shoppers with their Thalhimers bags and boxes bustled around us, always lingering awhile to admire the magically animated window displays.

The minute my sisters and I walked through those big glass entrance doors, we were showered with attention. The sales clerks all knew us and would pat us on our heads while telling us how much we had grown. To our delight, the bakery workers gave us as many chocolate leaf-shaped cookies as we wanted. Sometimes, while the sales ladies in the French Room were greeting Mom, we would crawl under the racks of wedding gowns and pick up beads and rhinestones that had fallen off so we could make bracelets with them. In the perfume department they would give us handfuls of little sample vials of whatever perfume we chose.

Above the first-floor elevator doors hung pictures of our ancestors—the past store presidents. I recall thinking how much they looked like my own Grandpa and how proud they would be if they could see his success. He helped Thalhimers grow from a tiny dry-goods shop to a huge department store selling everything imaginable.

Shoppers in the downtown store could choose from an unusual variety of departments. Not only did Thalhimers offer housewares, makeup, menswear, and shoes, but engraved stationery, stamps and coins, oriental rugs, toys, furs and a smoke shop, too. There was even a travel agent, an optician, a beauty parlor, a pharmacy, and a bridal salon. Restaurant choices included the men's Soup Bar, the deli and bakery, the fancy Richmond Room, and Angelos, a hot dog joint in the basement that had jukeboxes at every booth. The store felt like one big playground for my sisters and me.

We always met Daddy at his office on the fifth floor, just past the old Thalhimers delivery wagon on display. If Daddy still had work to do, we would play with the little Snow Bears and

Downtown Thalhimers where Daddy
and Snow Bear went every day

Tiny versions of the Thalhimer shopping bag
and bakery box for our dollhouse

other toys he kept in his closet. His secretaries would let us sit at their desks and play with their typewriters, where we promptly went through a substantial amount of store stationery. When Dad was ready, we headed to the highlight of our day—the Snow Bear Breakfast.

We met Grandma and Grandpa in the Richmond Room, where we were seated among other excited children and their families. After we ate our scrambled eggs, bacon, and grits, we joined in singing boisterous holiday tunes. When Bruce, the singer at every Breakfast, led everyone in a round of "Here Comes Santa Claus," we knew the moment had finally arrived! If we were loud enough, Santa would show up to the cheers of all the children in the restaurant. As we excitedly bellowed "Here Comes Snow Bear," our favorite cuddly friend would come bounding in, greeted with squeals of glee and enormous applause. Santa and Snow Bear visited each table, handing out lollipops and stickers to everyone. Then they joined all of us in singing and dancing around the piano. We would giggle for hours after this frenzy of fun.

After breakfast we visited the Winter Wonderland, a spacious room transformed into a holiday delight for the senses. "Frosty the Snowman" echoed throughout while tiny animated characters sang and frolicked around their wintry world. The scent of candy canes wafted in the air as we followed the winding paths around the magical, icicle-covered room to Santa's chair. Some years Santa knew exactly what we wanted for Christmas before we even said a word! Snow Bear was ever present as Santa's "right hand bear," and children flocked to him for hugs and pictures. Some kids were afraid of Santa, but no one was ever afraid of Snow Bear.

Then we stopped by "Snow Bear's Hibernation Station," which was a shop shaped like a big igloo. Only children were allowed inside, making it a very special privilege. With Snow Bear's help, everyone selected gifts for their moms and dads from an array of picture frames, wallets, gloves, key chains, and other small accessories. Being able to shop by ourselves made us feel so grown up.

When I was sixteen years old, Thalhimers was sold. I attended my last Snow Bear Breakfast and bought my last gifts from the Hibernation Station. Letting go of a part of my childhood tugged at my heartstrings, and I somehow knew it was the end of an era. I remember being sad that I would never work at Thalhimers and that my childhood dream to be the first woman store president would never come true. I remember eating my last popover in the Richmond Room and saying goodbye to the waitresses.

I remember wondering where we would buy our clothes since we had never really shopped anywhere else. And I remember crying when we stood outside the entrance of our store for one last picture, right before they took down the "Thalhimers" sign.

Going downtown for the holidays is no longer a family tradition, and Santa has long since moved to the mall. But Snow Bear lives on, carrying the spirit and magic of times gone by. He reminds me that I will always treasure my memories of Thalhimers and all of the people there that made the store so special. And he will keep his spot on my bookshelf until I can someday share our stories with my own children. —S.E.T.

Saying good-bye to Thalhimers the day they took
the sign down (even Snow Bear came along)

# Our Snow Bear Memories

Albums save memories
Of moments we share;
This one holds times
With my favorite bear.

My favorite bear

His name is Snow Bear, he lived in our store,

Where he happily frolicked from floor to floor.

Going to see him would fill us with glee—

What a magical time for my sisters and me.

Visiting young Snow Bear with our mommy

Daddy and Snow Bear

Went downtown each day,

Where Daddy would work

While Snow Bear would play!

Daddy holding his Snow Bear

Dressed in red overalls, big shoes with red laces,

His antics brought smiles to everyone's faces.

Amidst shoes and hats and dresses so new,

He entertained workers and customers, too.

Snow Bear the showbear!

At Christmas, our favorite memory by far

Was Breakfast with Snow Bear, where he was the star.

While happily singing a holiday song,

We giggled as Snow Bear would dance right along.

Snow Bear dancing while Bruce sings

In the Richmond Room, we gathered to eat—

Even for Grandpa, it was a special treat.

From table to table our Snow Bear would go

Making friends with the children, their faces aglow.

Snow Bear loved Grandpa, too

Snow Bear visited us every Christmas Day;

While my whole family sang, the piano he'd play.

Always the star, Snow Bear took center stage,

Spreading laughter to everyone of every age.

What a talented bear!

When we were little

We loved to pretend

To have tea parties

With our furry fun friend.

A pretend Snow Bear tea party

Because he was so loved, he quickly became

The bear in the spotlight—surrounded by fame.

There were pictures of him on clothes, mugs, books, and toys,

And fluffy stuffed Snow Bears for girls and for boys.

Snow Bear and "son"

Due to his fortune and due to his fame,

Our bear could help others by lending his name—

From Childrens' Hospital to the Christmas Mother

He shared his big heart, and he loved like no other.

Snow Bear lends a helping hand

As we're getting older, year after year,

Our fondness for Snow Bear grows even more dear.

The store may have closed, but the memories are there

Still kept alive by our favorite bear.

Growing up together

He's huggable, lovable, kind beyond measure—

A magical pal, a most precious treasure.

Changes are constant, things come and they go,

But the friendship of Snow Bear we'll never outgrow.

Friends forever

# Snow Bear's Favorite Recipes

*(Recipes reminiscent of Thalhimer's Richmond Room, Sword and Kilt Restaurants, Catering Service, Food Markets, Soup Bar, and Bakeries)*

# Buttered Pecans

2 pounds pecan halves
1 stick of butter
Garlic salt or plain salt (to taste)

Place pecans on roasting pan. Melt butter and pour over pecans. Put in oven at 225 degrees for approximately 1½ hours. Stir occasionally. Put pecans on paper towels and salt immediately while hot.

*"When Thalhimers catered our parties, these were served in little crystal bowls on the bar."*

# Marinated Shrimp

I cup vegetable oil
I cup cider vinegar
¼ cup capers and juice
½ teaspoon salt (optional)
⅛ teaspoon pepper
¼ cup sugar
3 medium yellow onions, sliced thin
Juice of one lemon

I bay leaf
½ teaspoon garlic powder
¼ teaspoon dry mustard
½ teaspoon parsley flakes
I teaspoon Worcestershire sauce
3 pounds shrimp, cooked and deveined
1 6-oz. can black olives

Combine all ingredients except shrimp and olives. Blend well. Add shrimp and olives and marinate in refrigerator at least 2 hours (up to 2 days is okay). Turn often. Have toothpicks for serving.

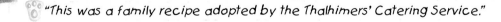

*"This was a family recipe adopted by the Thalhimers' Catering Service."*

# Tomato Bacon Cheese Bites

3 medium-sized red tomatoes
1 pound sharp grated cheddar cheese
4-5 slices of bacon
1 stick of butter or margarine
1 loaf of thin sliced white bread
Garlic salt

Peel and dice tomatoes. Drain. Season with garlic salt. Butter bread and cut into rounds with a cookie cutter. Put tomatoes, then grated cheese on the bread rounds. Slice bacon into thin pieces and put on top. Place on baking sheet in oven at 250 degrees for about 15 minutes. Put under the broiler for a few minutes at end (watching at all times). Broil until bacon is crisp. Cool and serve.

*"Always a hit at Thalhimers parties, these were served on silver trays by the waiters."*

# Water Chestnuts Wrapped in Bacon

1 pound sliced bacon
3 cans whole water chestnuts
1/4 cup brown sugar
1/4 cup Colman's dry mustard

Cut bacon slices into thirds. Sprinkle with brown sugar and Colman's mustard. Wrap bacon around each water chestnut and secure with a wooden toothpick. Broil until bacon is crisp on all sides.

*"A yummy appetizer served at store and family parties - including Thanksgiving!"*

# Deviled Crabs

1 pound crabmeat, carefully picked
1 teaspoon each: prepared yellow mustard, prepared horseradish
1/4 cup mayonnaise (approximately)
1 egg beaten
Tabasco - season to taste
Paprika

Preheat oven to 350 degrees. In a large bowl, gently mix crabmeat, mustard, horseradish, eggs, and Tabasco sauce. Add just enough mayonnaise to hold mixture together. Divide into 8 portions and pack lightly into cleaned crab shells or ramekins. Dust with paprika. Bake on top oven rack until lightly browned, 10-15 minutes.

*"Daddy used to bring these home from the Thalhimers' Deli for summertime dinners."*

# Chicken Salad

2 cups cubed cooked chicken breast
2 cups finely chopped celery
2 tablespoons freshly squeezed lemon juice
1/2 cup Hellman's mayonnaise (no substitute)
White pepper and salt to taste

In a large bowl, combine chicken, celery, lemon juice, and mayonnaise. Stir to blend. Add pepper and salt. Mix thoroughly. Chill before serving.

*"Served in sandwiches or on a bed of lettuce at Thalhimers' Food Markets and Sword & Kilt Restaurants."*

# Chinese Slaw

**Noodle Mix** - Toast at 250 degrees for 15 minutes and set aside:

2 packages beef flavored Ramen Noodle Soup, crushed
1 cup sunflower seeds
1 cup slivered almonds

**Dressing** - Can make ahead. Heat until dissolved:

1/3 cup white vinegar
1/2 cup (or less) sugar

Then add: 1 cup oil
2 packages seasonings from Raman noodles (beef flavor)

**Salad:**

1 pound package cole slaw mix
1 bunch green onions, sliced thin (or chopped onion)
2 carrots, grated
Red cabbage, chopped (optional)

Add noodle mix and dressing to salad just before serving. Toss.

*"Reminiscent of the Chinese Chicken Salad we loved in the Richmond Room."*

# Potato Salad

8 small new potatoes
1 medium onion, minced
1/2 cucumber, peeled and diced
1/4 cup diced celery
2 tablespoons minced green pepper

1 tablespoon minced fresh parsley
1/4 cup French dressing
1 teaspoon lemon juice
1/4 cup mayonnaise
Salt and pepper to taste

Scrub potatoes and cook in boiling salted water, about 20 minutes. Drain, cool slightly, peel and cube and place in salad bowl. Add onion, cucumber, celery, green pepper, and parsley and mix lightly. In a small bowl, combine French dressing, lemon juice, and mayonnaise and pour over vegetables while potatoes are still warm. Season with salt and pepper. Mix well. Chill. Serves four.

*"Always a delicious treat in the Thalhimers' Deli boxed lunches."*

# Pimento Cheese

1/2 cup margarine
1 tablespoon flour
1 pound sharp Cheddar cheese, shredded
1 large green bell pepper, finely diced
1/2 cup chopped pimento
Optional: black pepper, cayenne pepper, diced onions

In a saucepan over medium heat, melt margarine. Add flour stirring constantly to keep from lumping. Continue stirring and cook until slightly thickened and pale golden. Remove from heat. Place cheese, bell pepper and pimento in a large bowl. Stir in flour mixture until completely blended. Season with optional ingredients if desired. Chill thoroughly before serving.

*"In the olden days, pimento cheese sandwiches were served to businessmen in the Men's Soup Bar."*

# Herb Soup with Shrimp

½ cup chopped onion
¼ cup chopped green pepper
¾ cup chopped mushrooms
2 tablespoons butter
1 tablespoon lemon juice
½ teaspoon basil
½ teaspoon powdered savory (optional)

¼ teaspoon tarragon
½ teaspoon pepper
1 can (10 ½ oz.) cream of mushroom soup
1 can (10 ½ oz) beef consommé
½ cup milk
1 ¼ cups cooked chopped shrimp

Sauté the onion, green pepper, and mushrooms in butter until onion is tender. Season with basil, savory, tarragon, salt, and pepper. Meanwhile, heat the mushroom soup, consommé, and milk together. Add shrimp. Then add the onion mixture. Simmer for five minutes or until shrimp is hot.

Note: This can be served hot or cold. Yield: 1 quart.

*"A savory Thalhimers' soup. Daddy loved it!"*

# Popovers

8 tablespoons vegetable oil, divided
2 cups all-purpose flour
6 eggs
3 cups whole milk, divided
1/2 teaspoon sugar
2 tablespoons baking powder*

*Thalhimers' chefs always insisted upon using
 Rumford baking powder for perfect popovers.

Set oven at 400 degrees. Pour 1 teaspoon oil in each of 24 (2 1/2 inch) muffin cups or popover pans and place in oven until oil sizzles. In bowl of electric mixer at medium speed, beat flour, eggs, 1 1/2 cups milk, sugar and baking powder for at least 15 minutes. Add remaining 1 1/2 cups milk and beat 5 minutes longer. Pour batter into sizzling hot oil in muffin cups, filling each cup half full. Bake in preheated oven until golden brown and popped, about 20 minutes (check at 15 minutes).

*"Our Richmond Room waitress knew these were our favorites
 and served them to us before we even ordered."*

# Sally Lunn Muffins

1 yeast cake
2 cups lukewarm water
6 teaspoons sugar
1 teaspoon salt
½ cup vegetable shortening
2 eggs
4 cups flour
Whole milk as needed

Grease 2 (12-cup) muffin tins with vegetable shortening; set aside. In a small bowl, dissolve yeast cake in lukewarm water. Add sugar and salt. In a large bowl, beat together shortening and eggs. Add yeast mixture. Gradually sift in flour. Add enough milk to make a dough that can be handled easily. Pull off bits of dough and pat into biscuit shapes. Place in prepared muffin tins. In a warm place, let rise 2 hours or until they double in size. Bake at 375 degrees until lightly browned, about 15 to 20 minutes.

*"The black and white checked Thalhimers' bakery boxes were often filled with these."*

# Spoonbread

¼ cup margarine, melted
¾ cup white cornmeal
1½ cups boiling water
½ cup all-purpose flour
Pinch of salt

1½ cups whole milk
4 eggs
½ teaspoon sugar
1½ teaspoons baking powder (Rumford*)

*The only baking powder that's works is Rumford, according to old Thalhimers' recipes.

Preheat oven to 350 degrees. Pour margarine into 8 inch square baking pan. Place cornmeal in a mixing bowl. Pour boiling water over. Mix well. Stir in flour, milk, eggs, sugar, baking powder, and salt. Beat with a wire whisk until smooth. Pour into prepared pan. Bake in preheated oven until firm and golden brown, 30-35 minutes. Makes 9 servings.

"Another Richmond Room specialty and a traditional Southern favorite."

# Cheese Cake

3 pounds cream cheese
3 cups sugar
6 eggs
1 tablespoon vanilla
Zwieback crackers - crumbled
1/2 cup sugar - to mix with Zwiebacks
Topping: 1 cup sour cream mixed with 1 teaspoon vanilla
Or strawberry or cherry pie fillings

Blend cream cheese and sugar in mixer until smooth. Add eggs and vanilla. Pour into a glass baking dish (if you want to cut into squares) or a cheesecake pan lined with Zwieback crackers and sugar. Place in oven at 200 degrees for one hour. Check to see if it is cooked by inserting a wooden toothpick in cake. If it comes out clean, it is done. After you take cake out of oven, spread sour cream and vanilla mixture on top and sprinkle some of the Zwieback crumbs over it. (Or use pie fillings as topping.)

"After our parties catered by the store, we always hoped there was some cheesecake left over!"

# Coconut Custard Pie

4 tablespoons butter, softened
3/4 cup granulated sugar
2 eggs
3/4 cup milk
3/4 cup coconut
1  9-inch unbaked pie shell

Cream butter and sugar. Add eggs and beat. Add milk and beat. Add coconut and stir to blend. Pour into pie shell and bake at 350 degrees for 20-30 minutes or until custard is set. (Bake just until a silver knife inserted one inch from side of crust comes out clean.)

*"A top seller in the Thalhimers' bakery."*

# Rice Pudding

1/2 cup uncooked regular rice
3 eggs
1 1/3 cups milk
1/2 cup sugar
1/3 cup butter
1/2 cup raisins (optional)
1/2 teaspoon nutmeg
1/2 teaspoon cinnamon
1 1/2 teaspoons vanilla

Cook the rice. Beat the eggs. Combine all ingredients and mix well.
Pour into a 9 x 9 inch pan. Bake at 300 degrees for 40 minutes.

*"A delight for kids and grown-ups alike in the Richmond Room."*

# Six Layer Chocolate Cake

**Yellow cake:**

8 oz. Crisco
3 cups sugar
6 eggs
4 cups flour
1 1/2 teaspoons baking powder
2 teaspoons salt
2 cups milk
2 teaspoons vanilla

Preheat oven to 350 degrees. Cream together the Crisco and sugar with a heavy duty mixer on a medium setting for about 2 minutes. Add the 6 eggs one at a time and beat until yellow disappears. Alternately mix in dry ingredients (salt, flour, and baking powder) with the milk, ending with the dry ingredients. Blend in 2 teaspoons vanilla. Pour batter into 2 jelly roll pans (about 17 inches long x 12 inches wide x 1 inch deep) filled 1/4 inch deep. Bake at 350 degrees for 20-30 minutes, checking for doneness after about 20 minutes. Let cake cool for several hours before frosting. Cut into 6 rectangular slices 8 inches long by 4 1/2 inches wide. Trim off any crispy outer edges. Frost.

# Six Layer Chocolate Cake (cont')

## Chocolate Icing:

1 1/2 cups boiling water
8 1/2 cups powdered sugar
8 (1 oz.) Hersheys chocolate squares-melted
2 1/4 teaspoons hot water

Slowly mix hot water into 8 1/2 cups of powdered sugar. Add the melted chocolate. Beat by hand until smooth. Add 2 1/4 teaspoons water. Beat again. Frost one layer of cake then put another layer on top and frost. Let it sit a minute to set or the layer may slip off. Repeat until all six layers are frosted. Frost top, sides and ends. Cake size should be 8 inches long by 4 1/2 inches wide and 4 inches tall. (Use any extra frosting on the extra cake pieces!)

*"This 'takes the cake' as the all-time favorite at the Thalhimers' bakery!"*

## A Snow Bear Hug to:

Jeanne Ancarrow

Kathy Albers

Mack Austin

Betty Bauder

Weldon Bradshaw

Ann Chenoweth

Susan Dixon

Robert Dietz

The Dietz Press

Bob Eason

Chris Ekberg

The "Dog Town Diners"

Sharon Fink

Jeff Gallegher

Connie Gottwald

Michael Hatcher

Mary Holland

Denise Howell

Laurie Israel

Kenny Kane

Steve Mann

Martin Agency

Nancy & Tom McCandlish

Bruce Miller

Sally Moxley

Kaki Nelson

Kate Parthemus

Francie Reed

Kay Remick

Richmond Times Dispatch

Rachel Ruderman

Quallity Bake Shop

Eleanor Rufty

Wert Smith

Kimberly Tetlow

Lisa Thalhimer

Barbara Thalhimer

Theatre IV

Mary Turpin

Chris Turpin

Virginia Historical Society

Virginia Museum of Fine Arts

Phil Whiteway

Mary Denny Wray

### AND TO:

Billy, Christie, and Katherine

Mimi and Pop
  (Eddie & Jack Brush)

...and Grandma and Grandpa